Designs for Relaxation

PIG

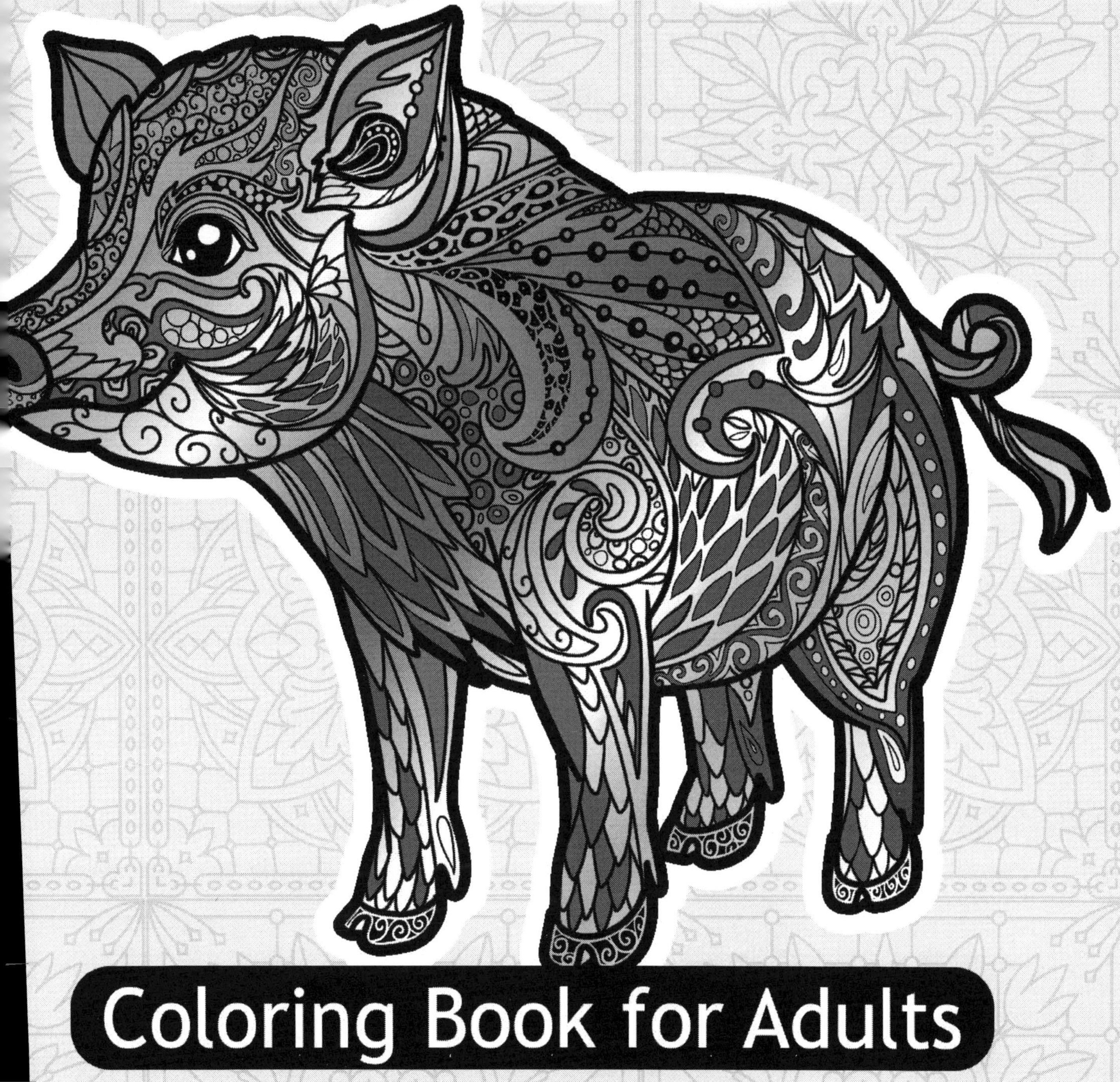

Coloring Book for Adults

TEST YOUR COLOR

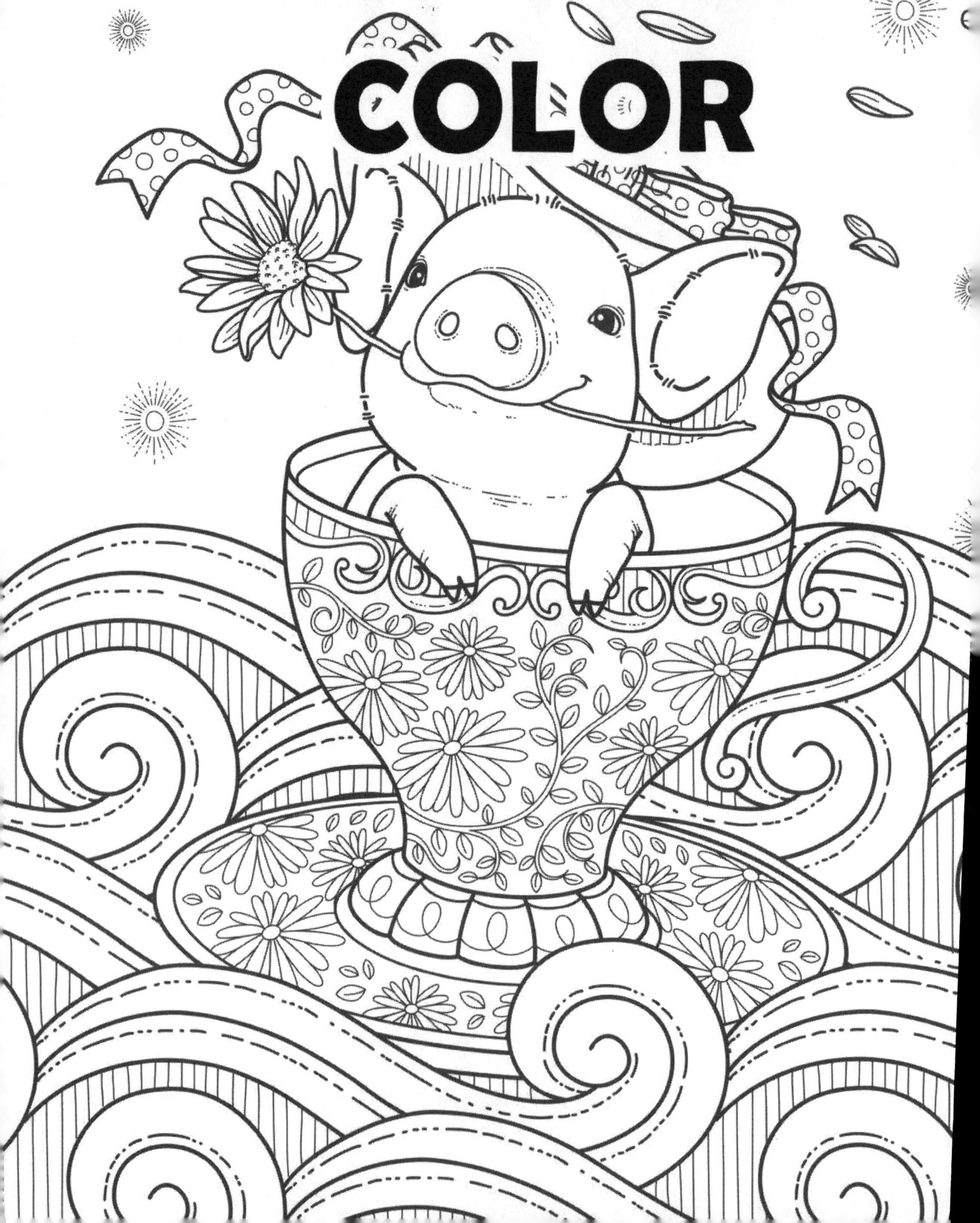

TEST YOUR COLOR

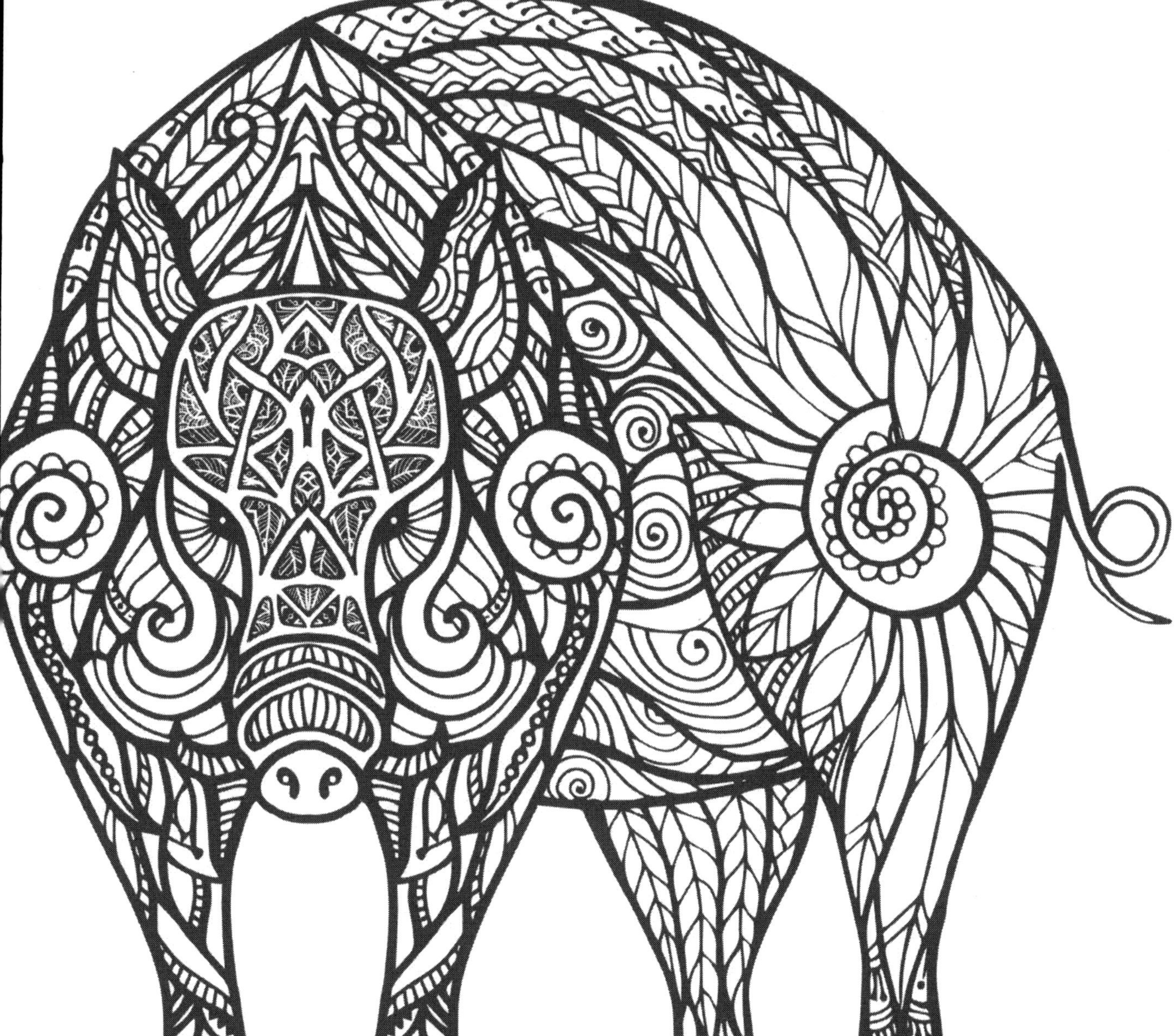

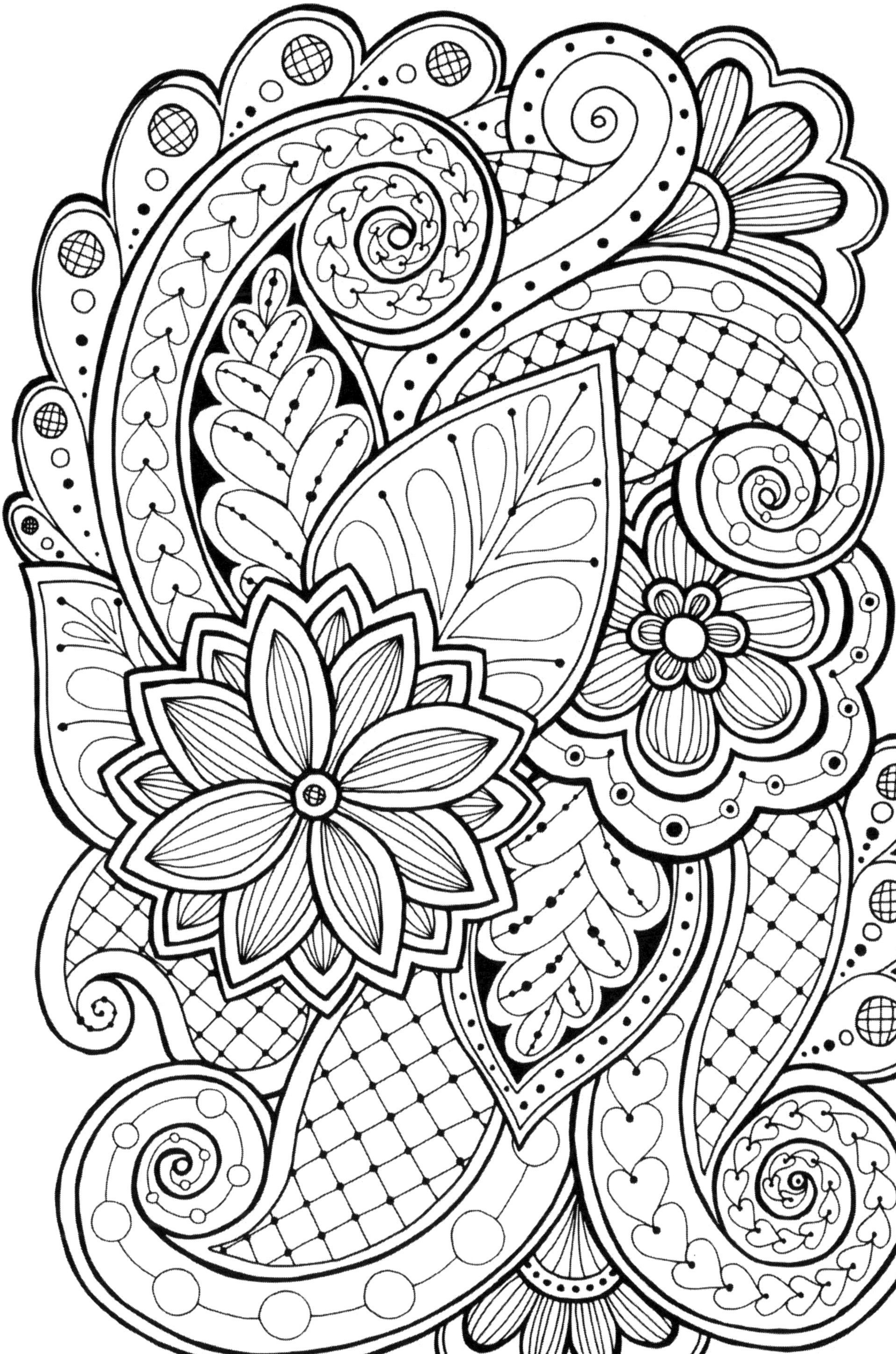

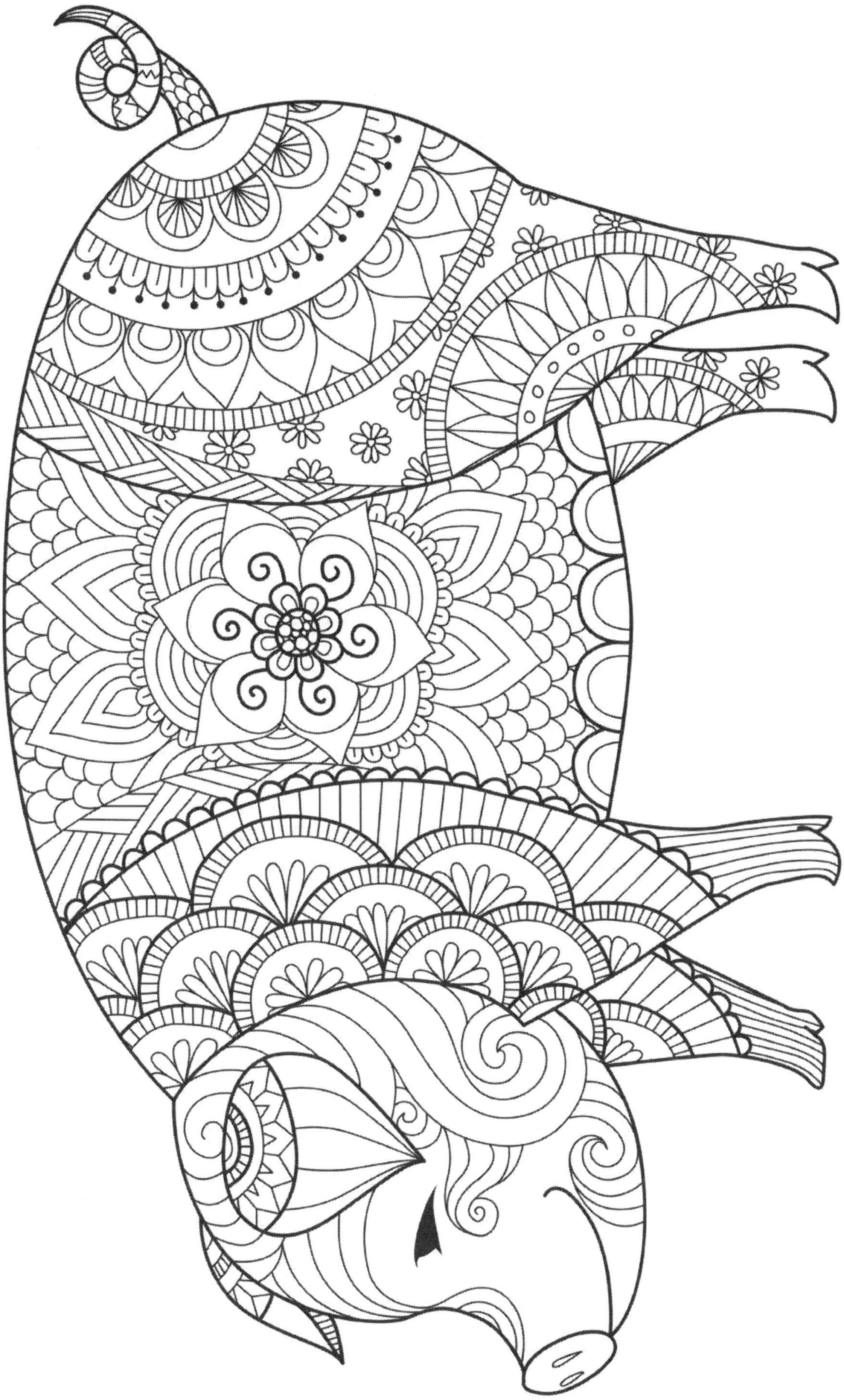

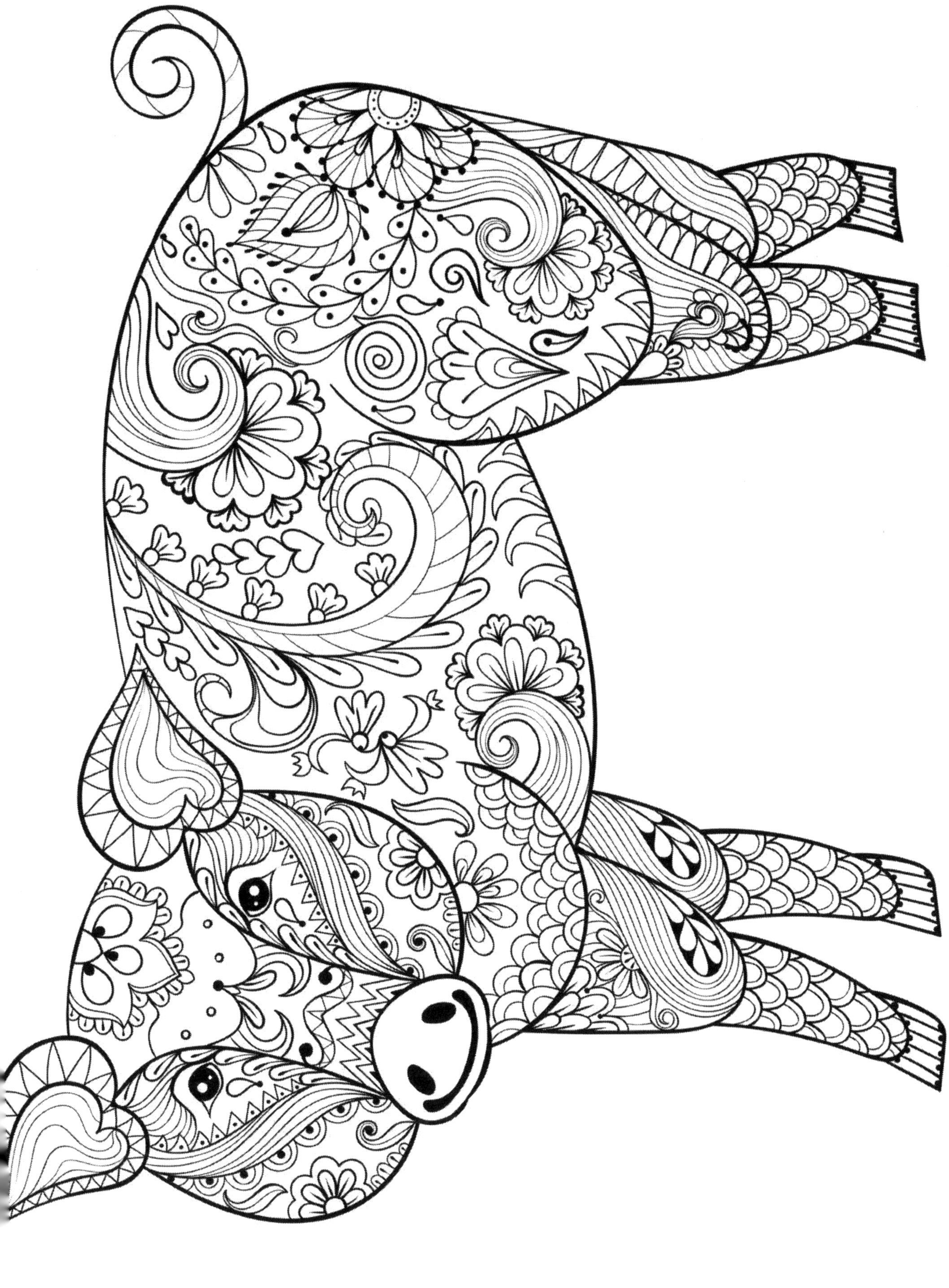

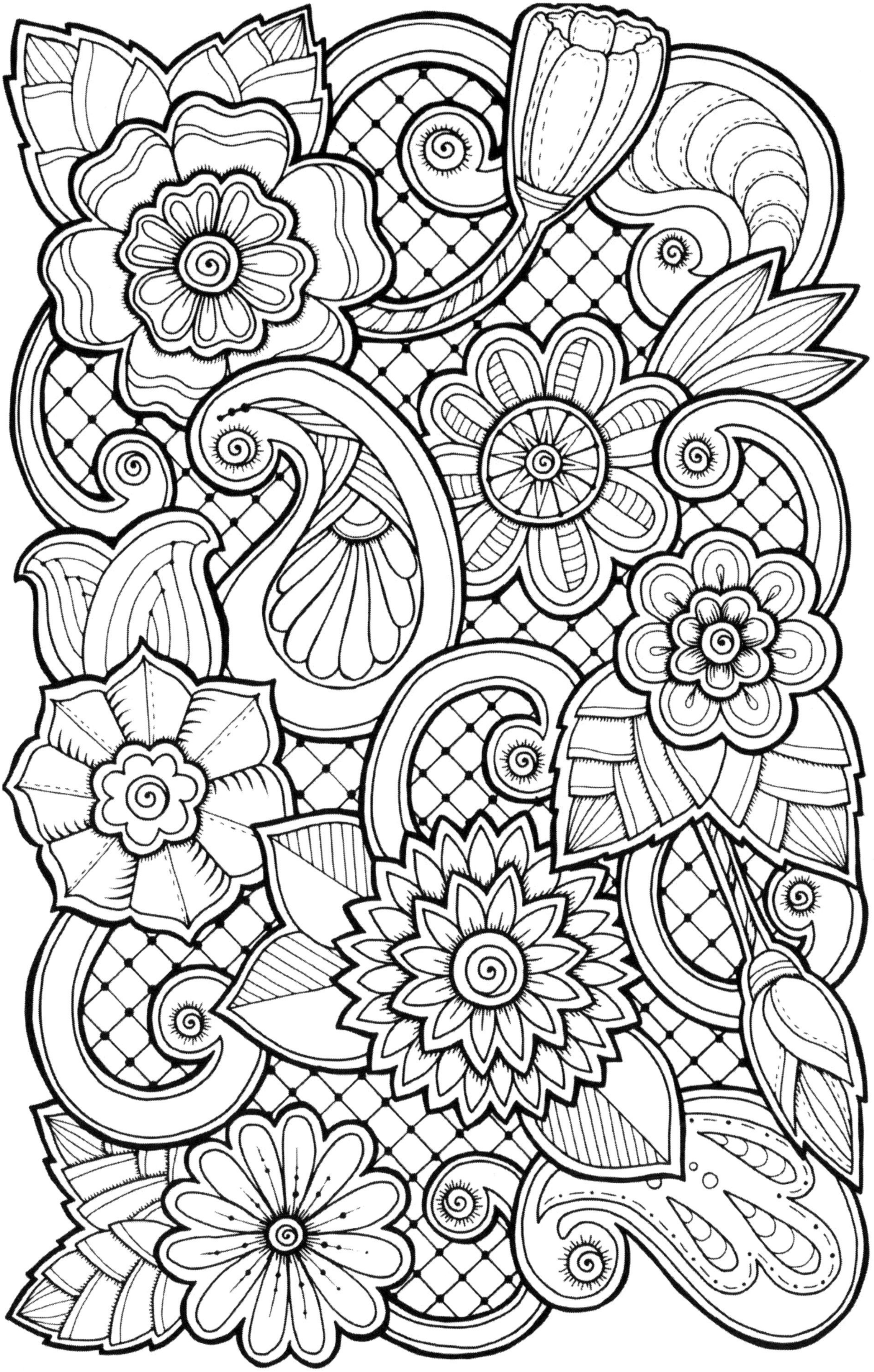

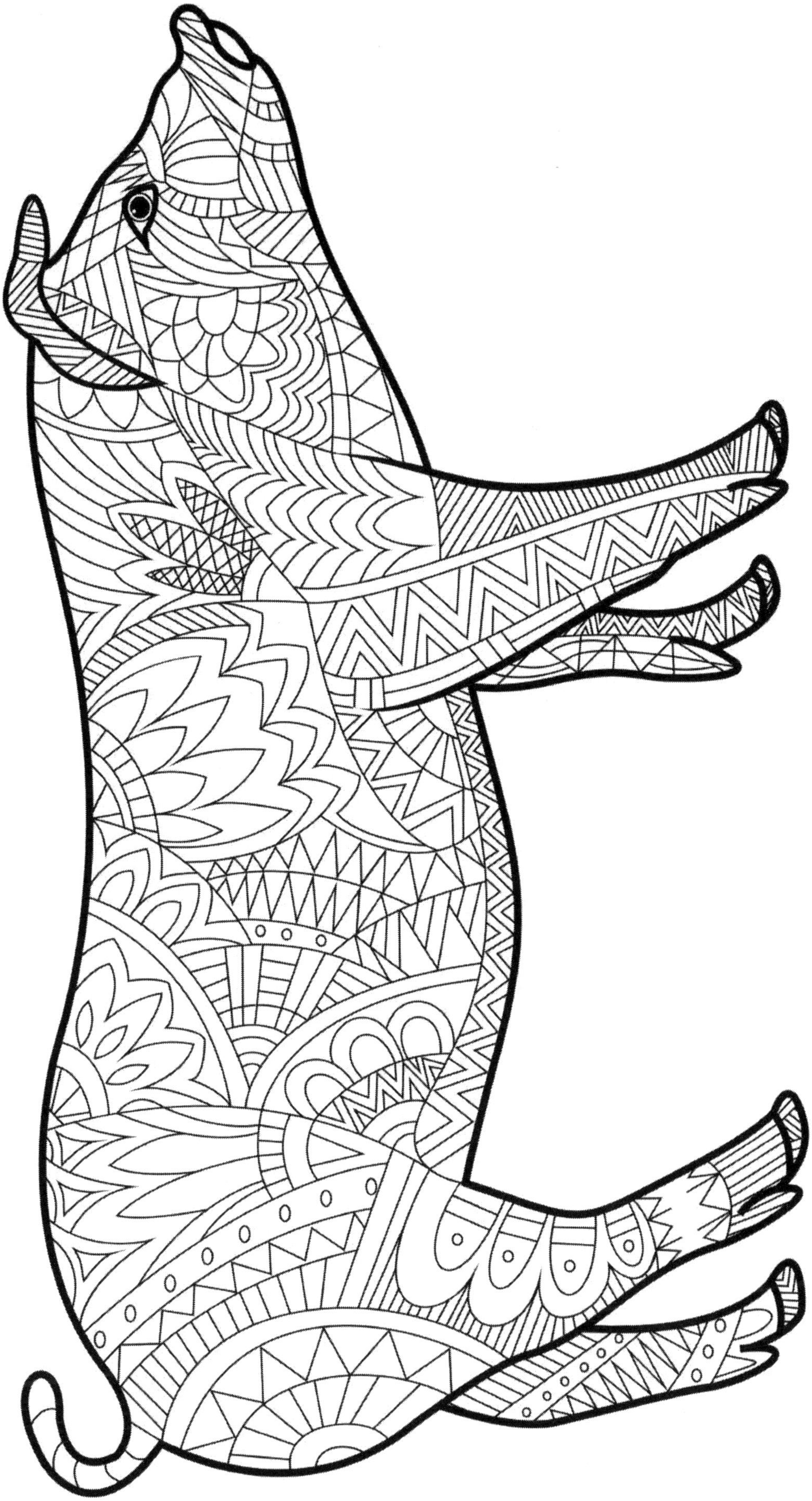

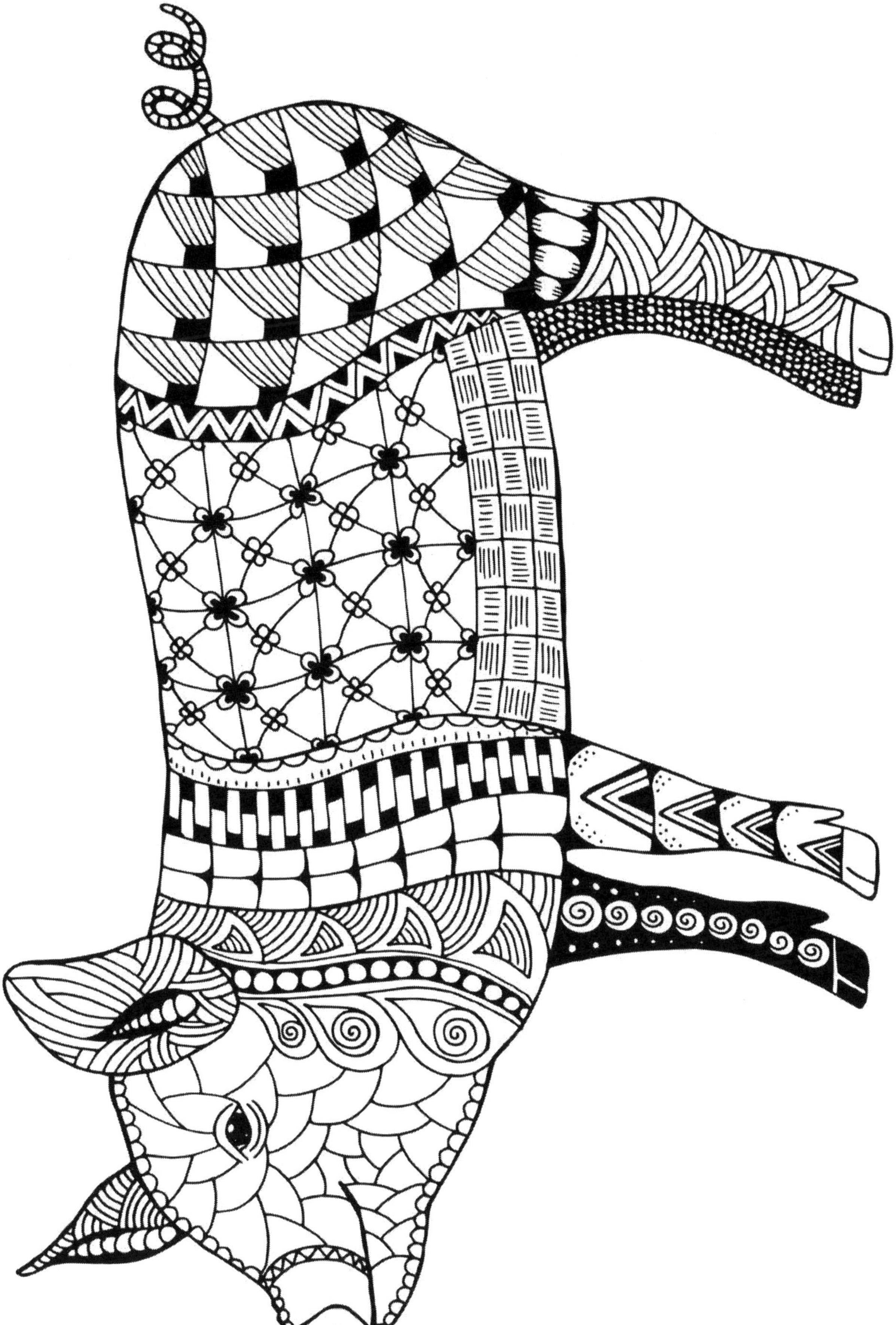

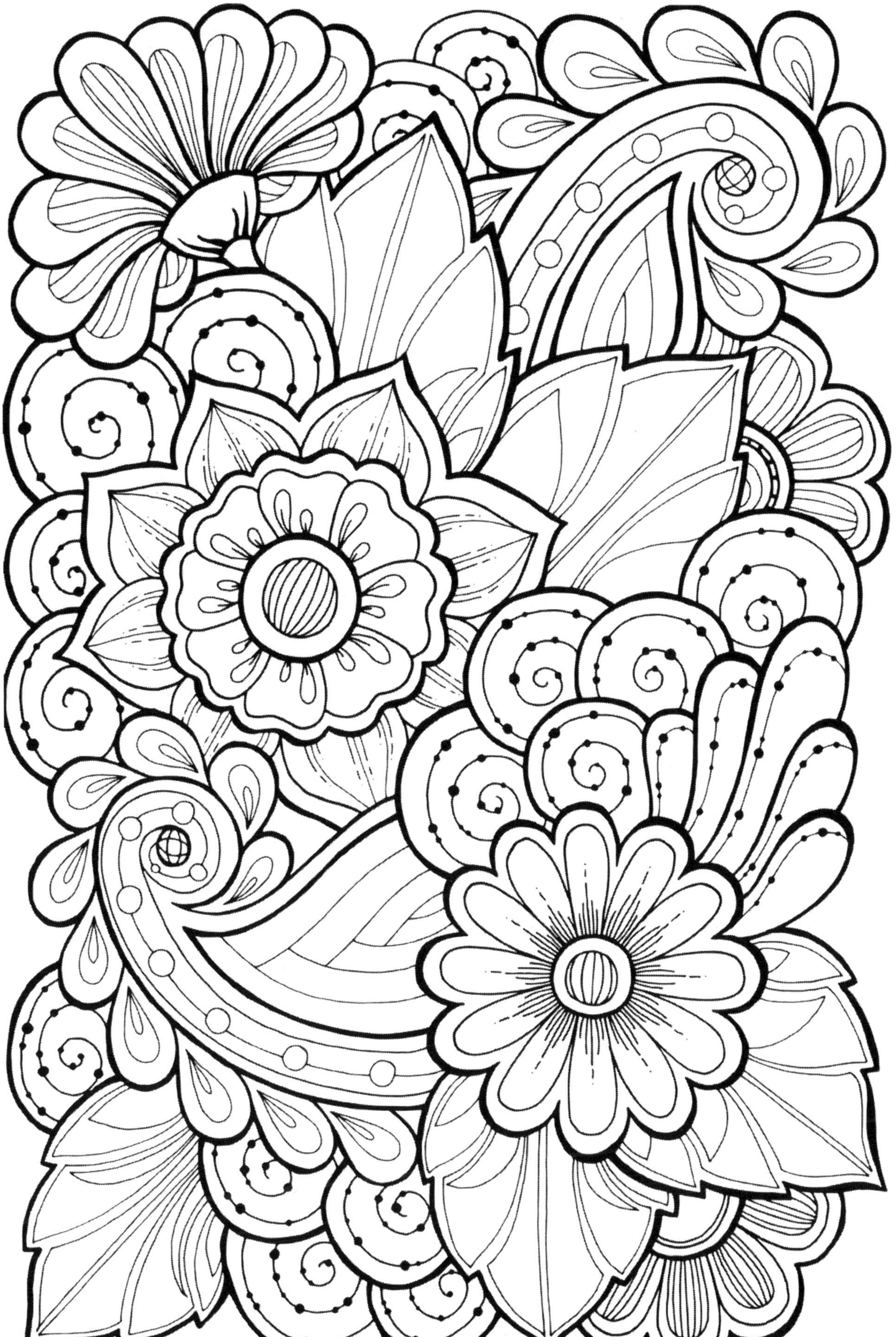

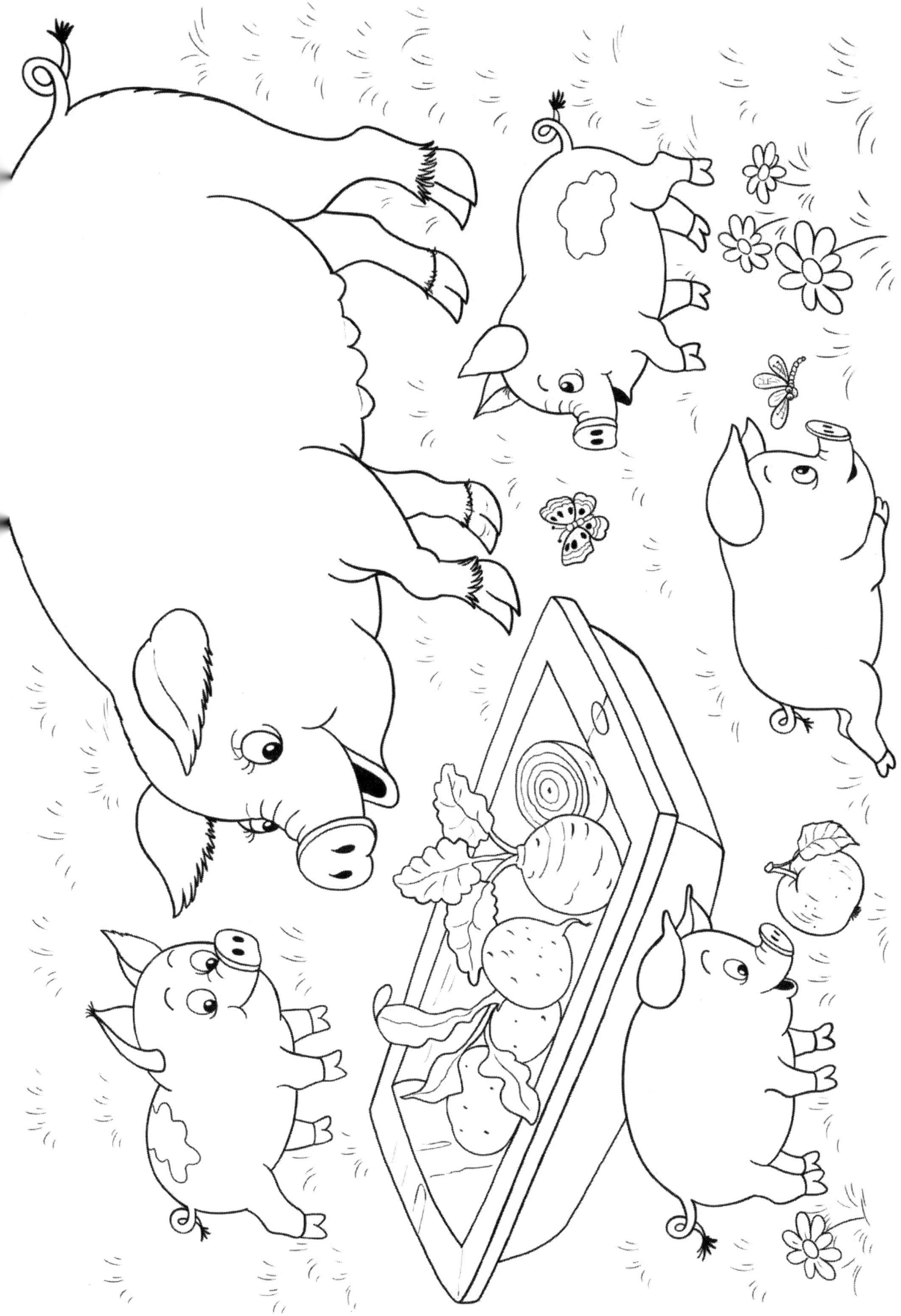

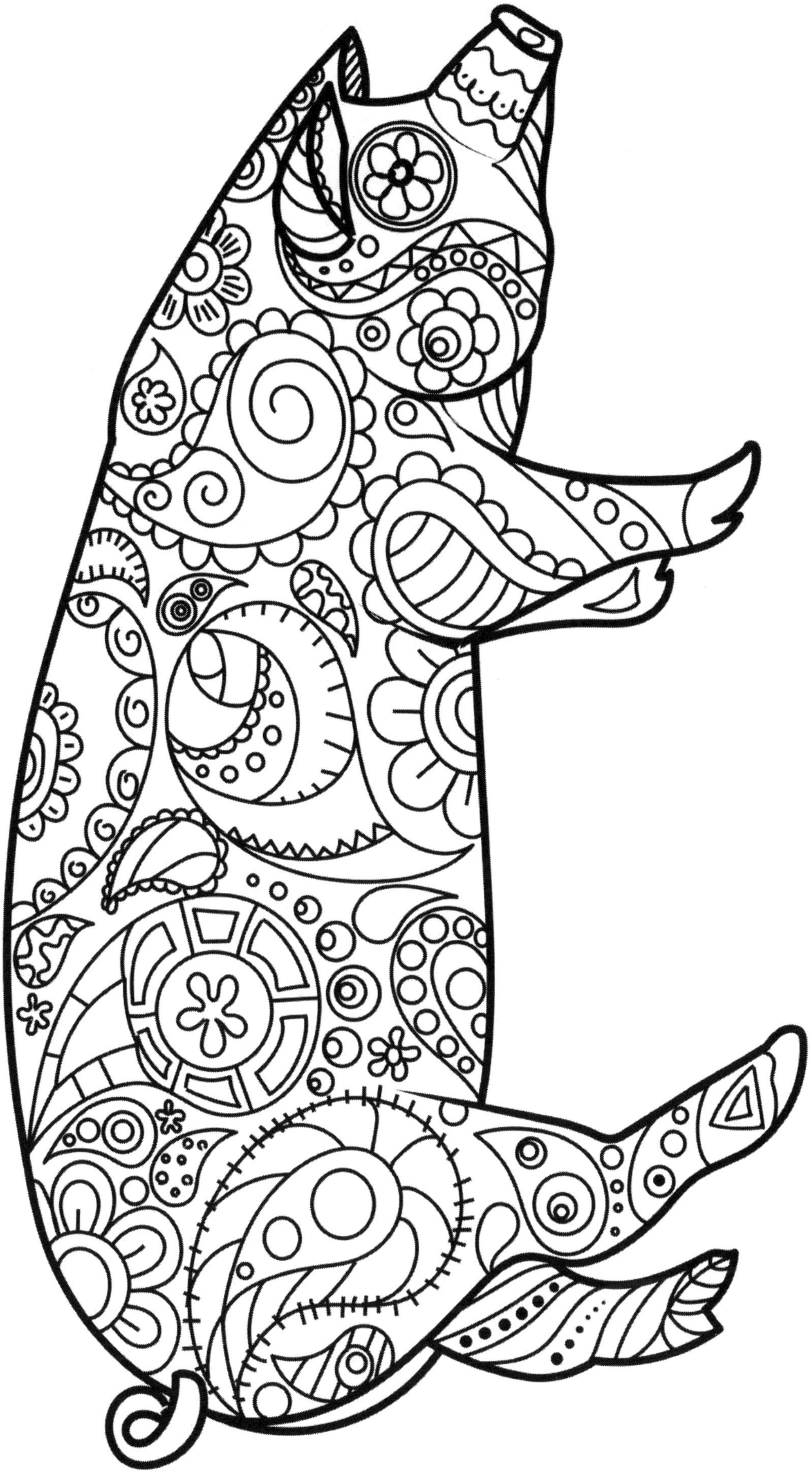

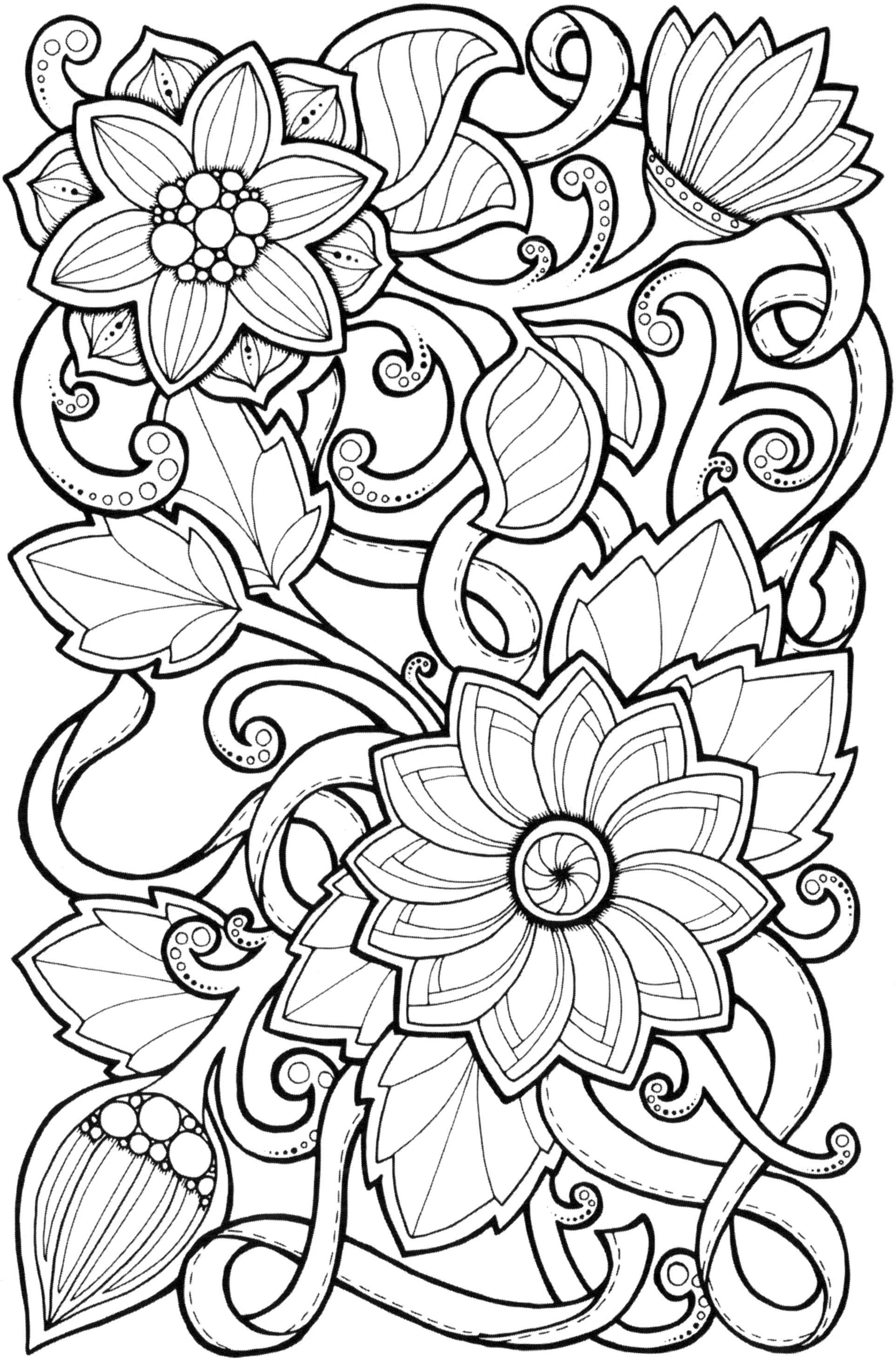

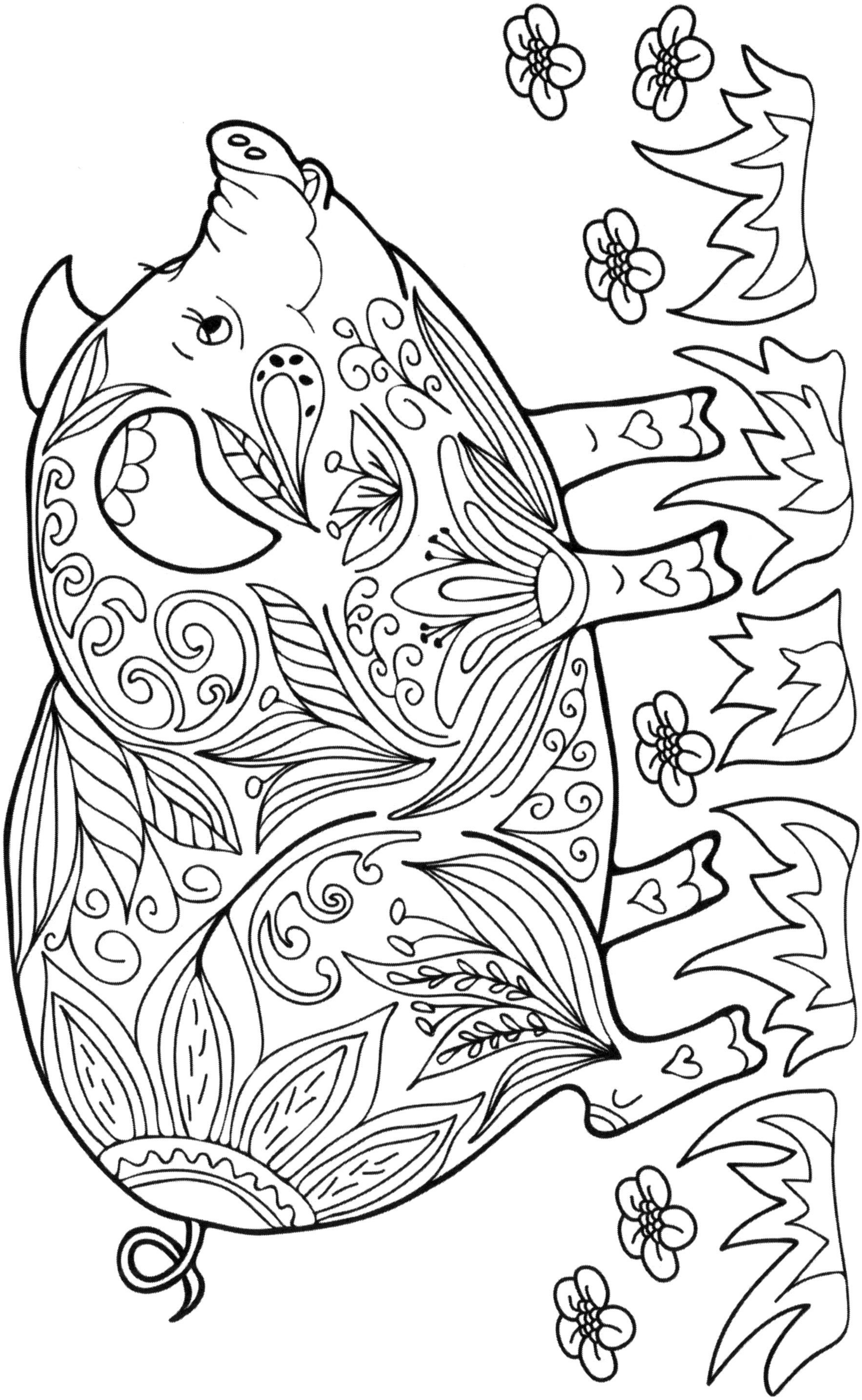

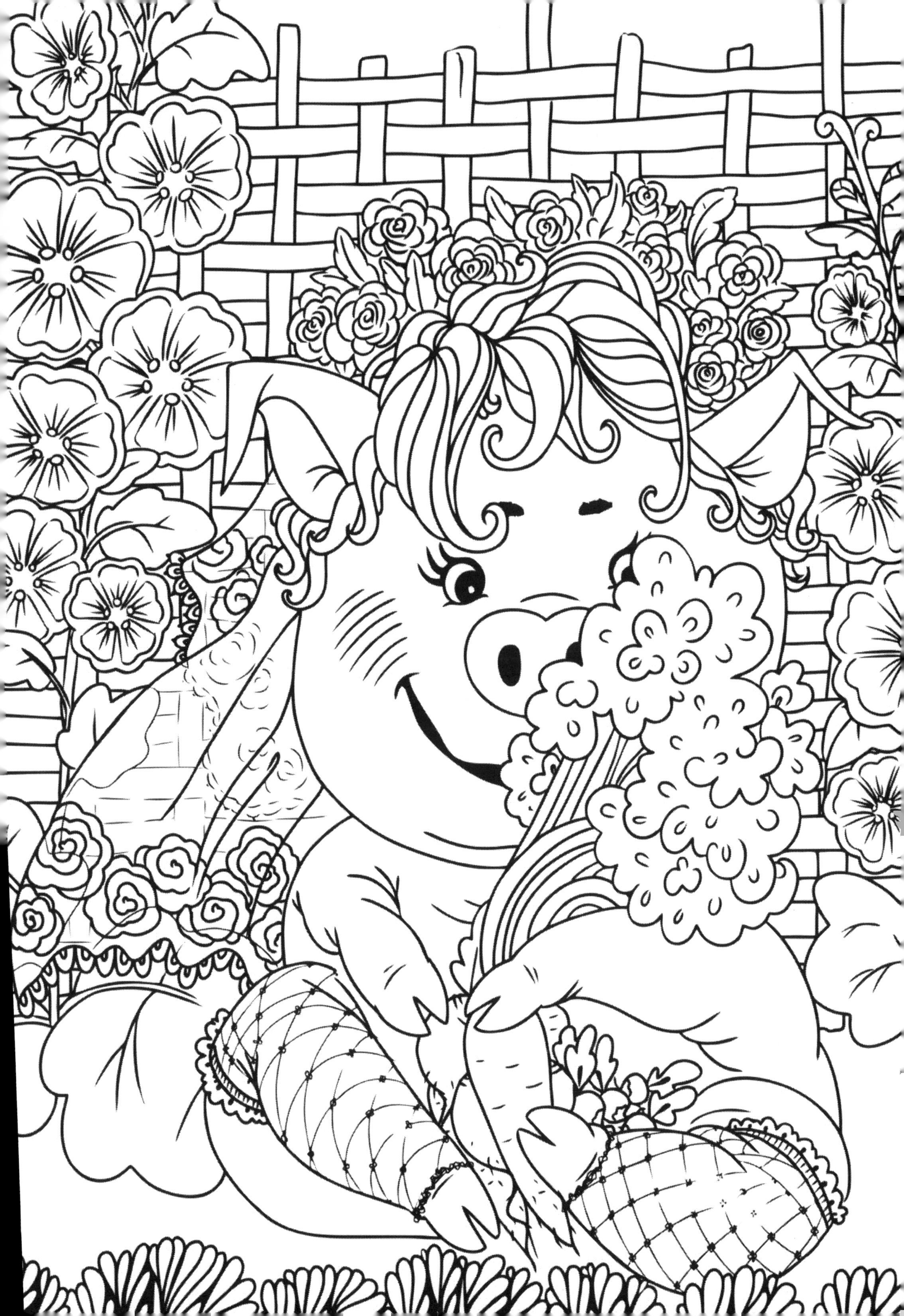

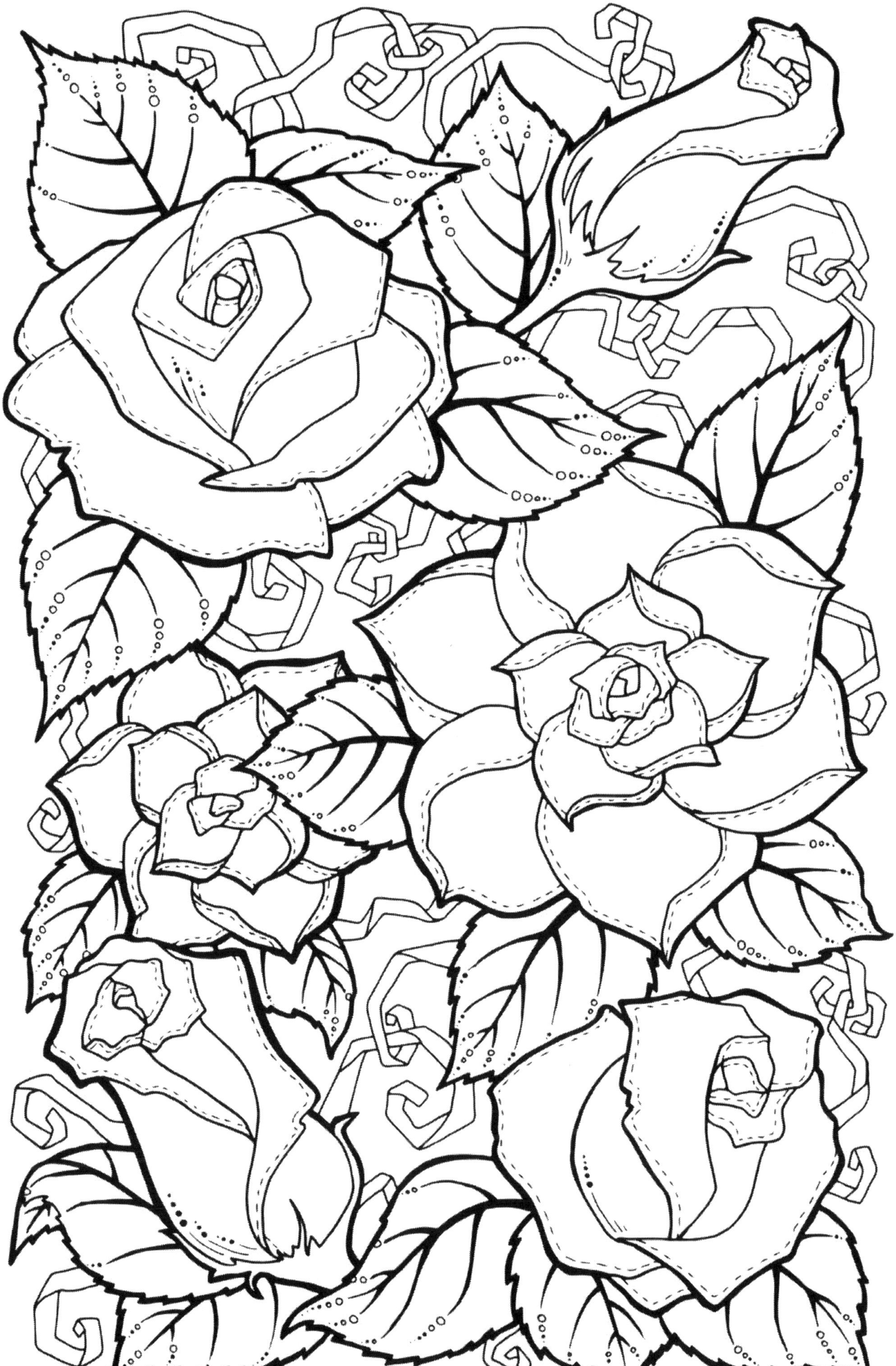

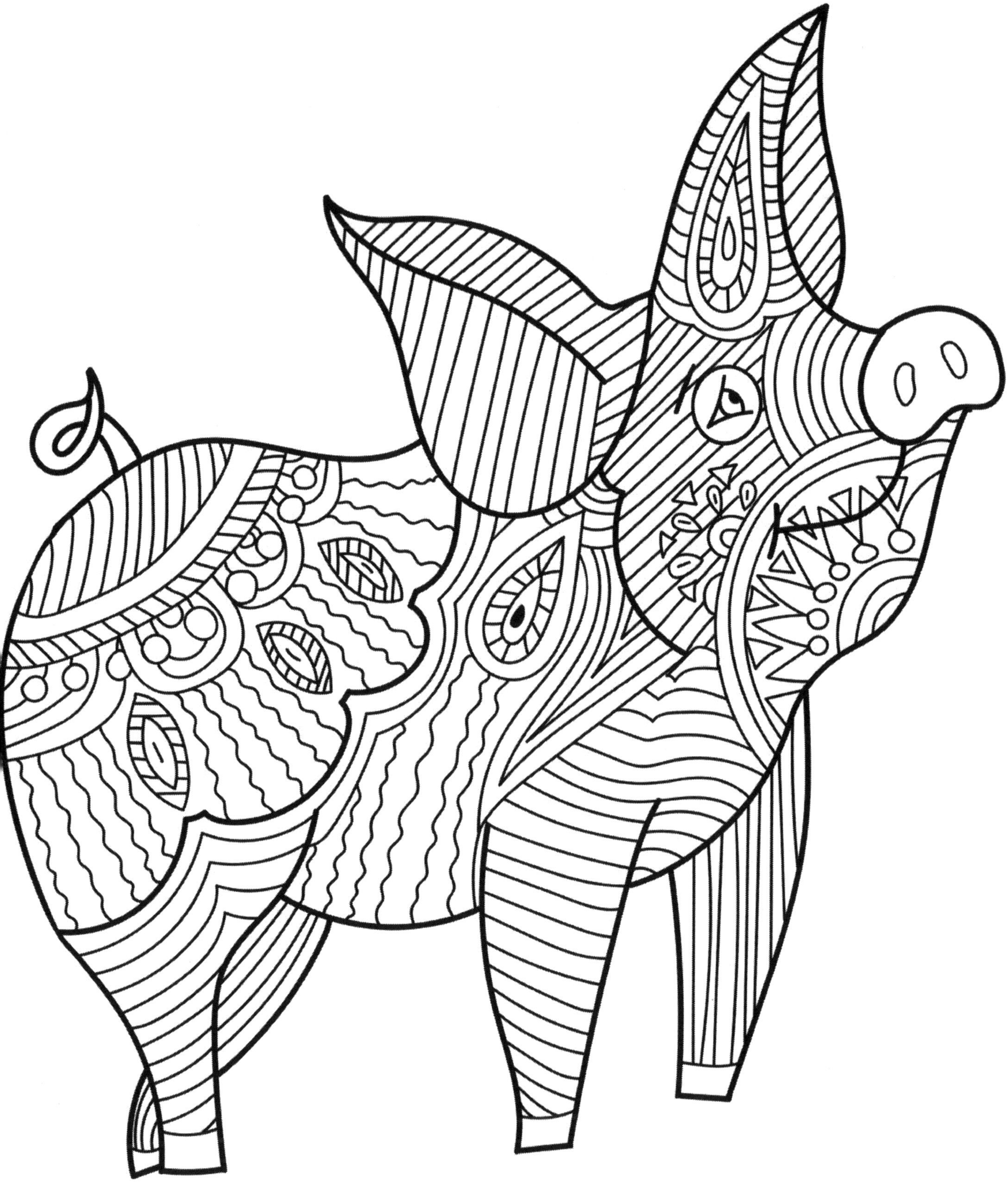

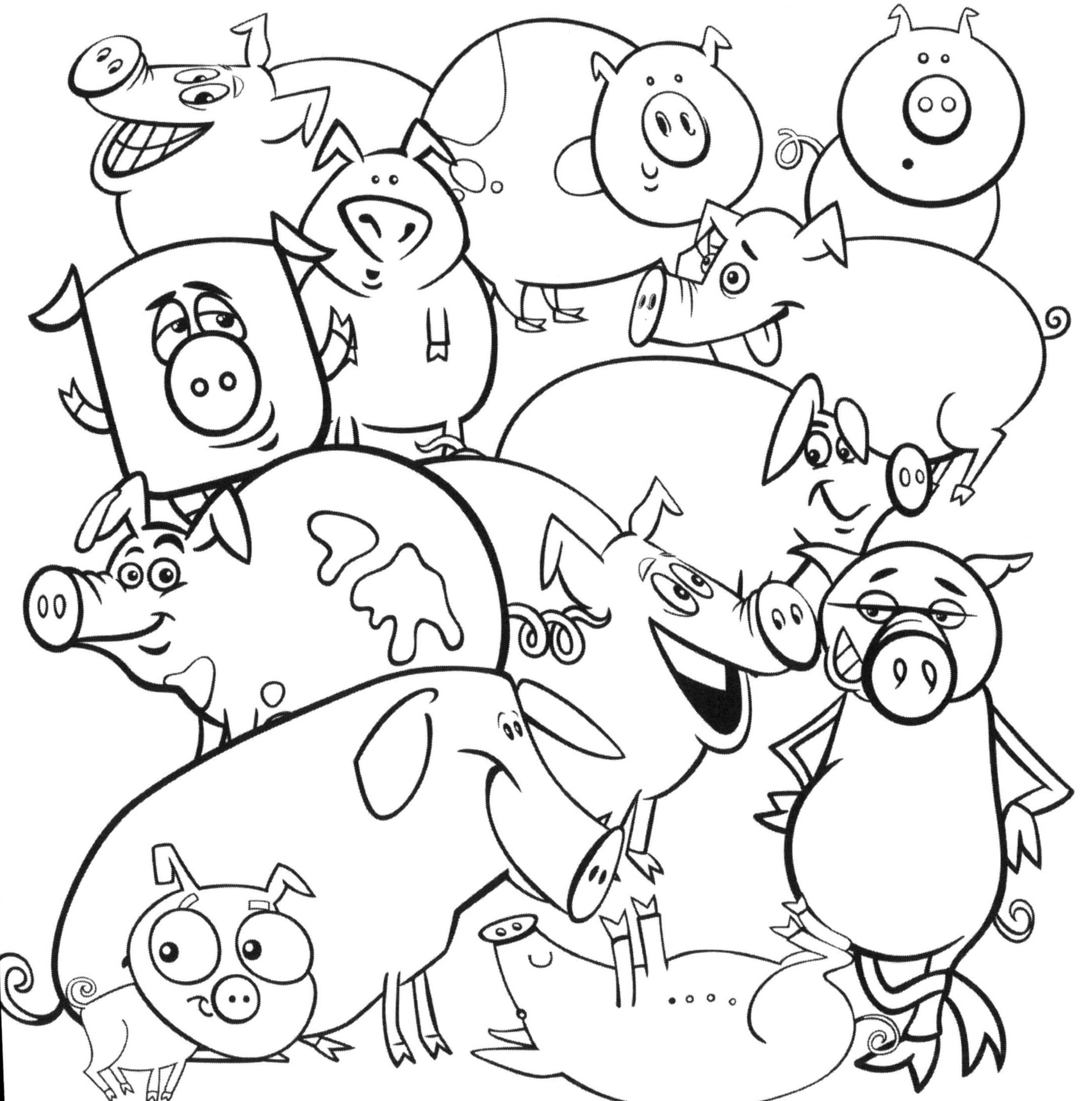

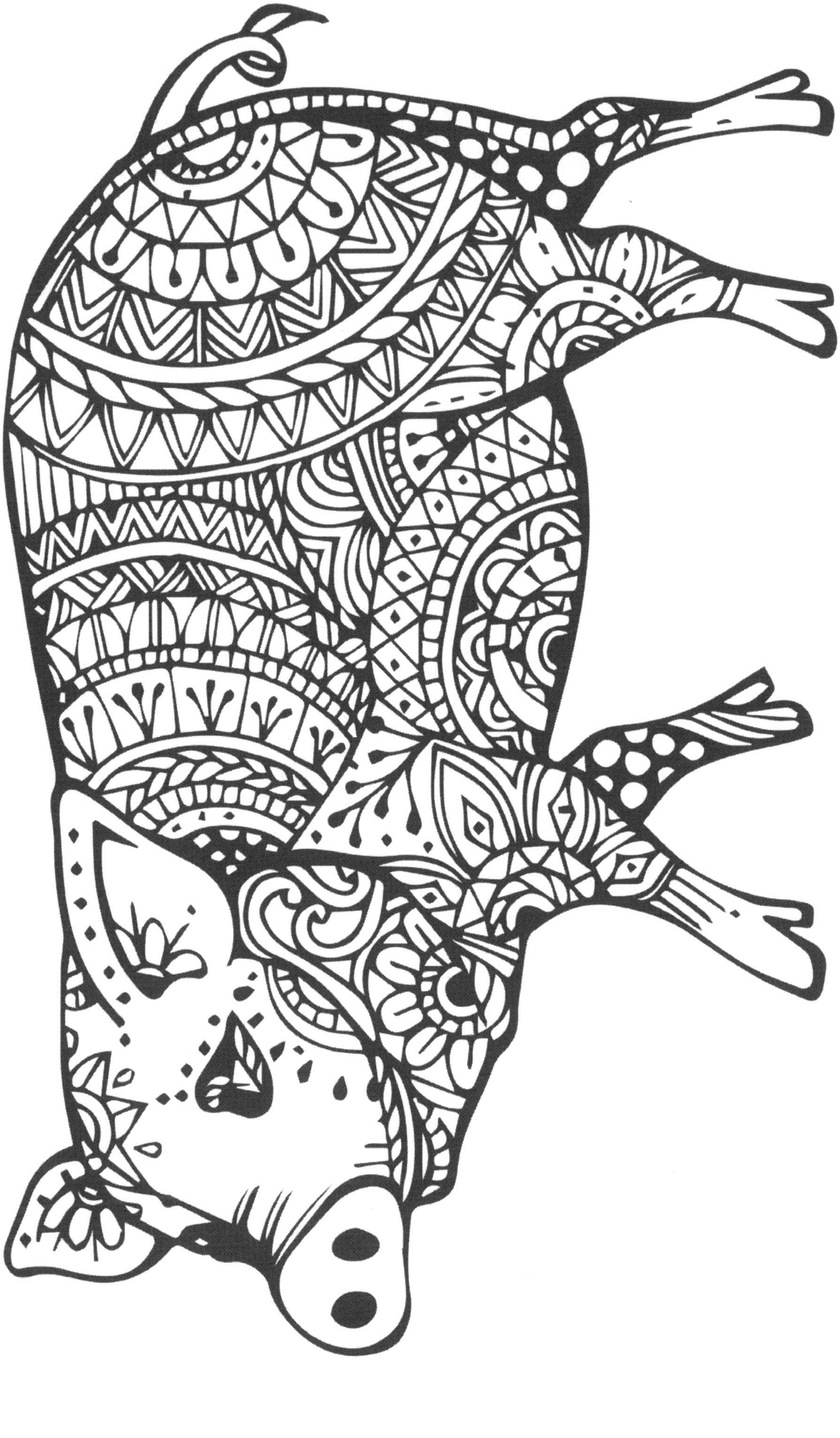

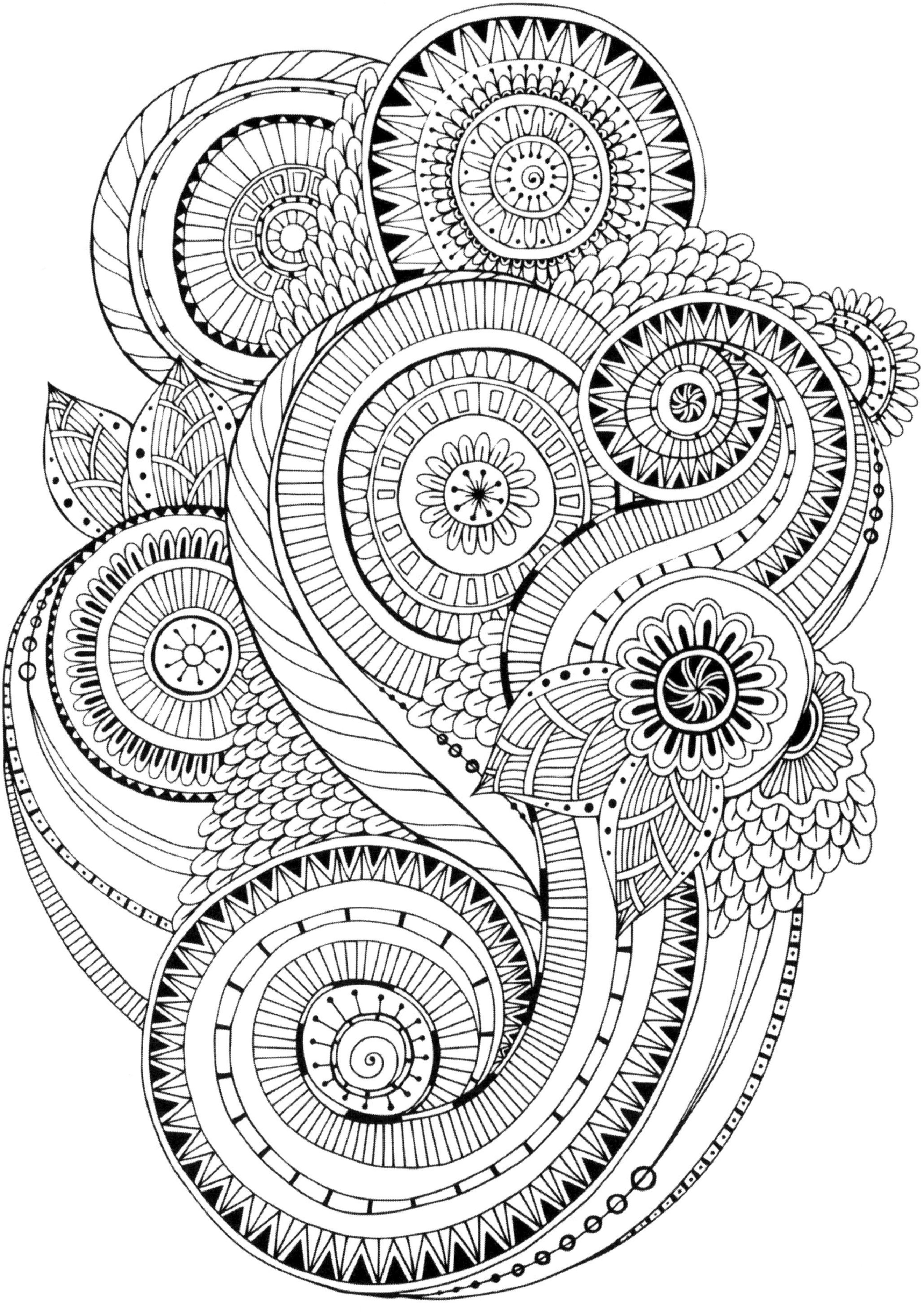

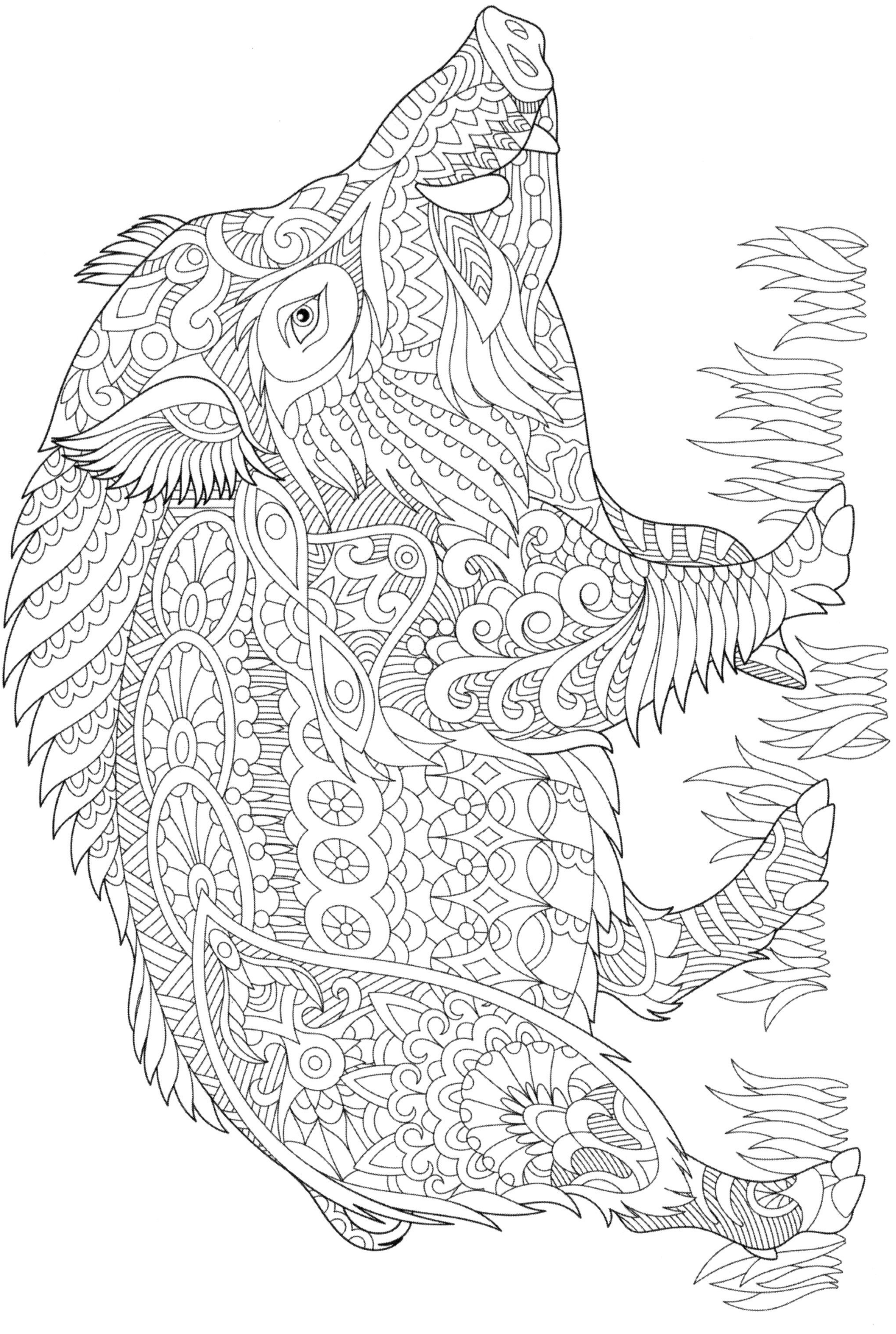

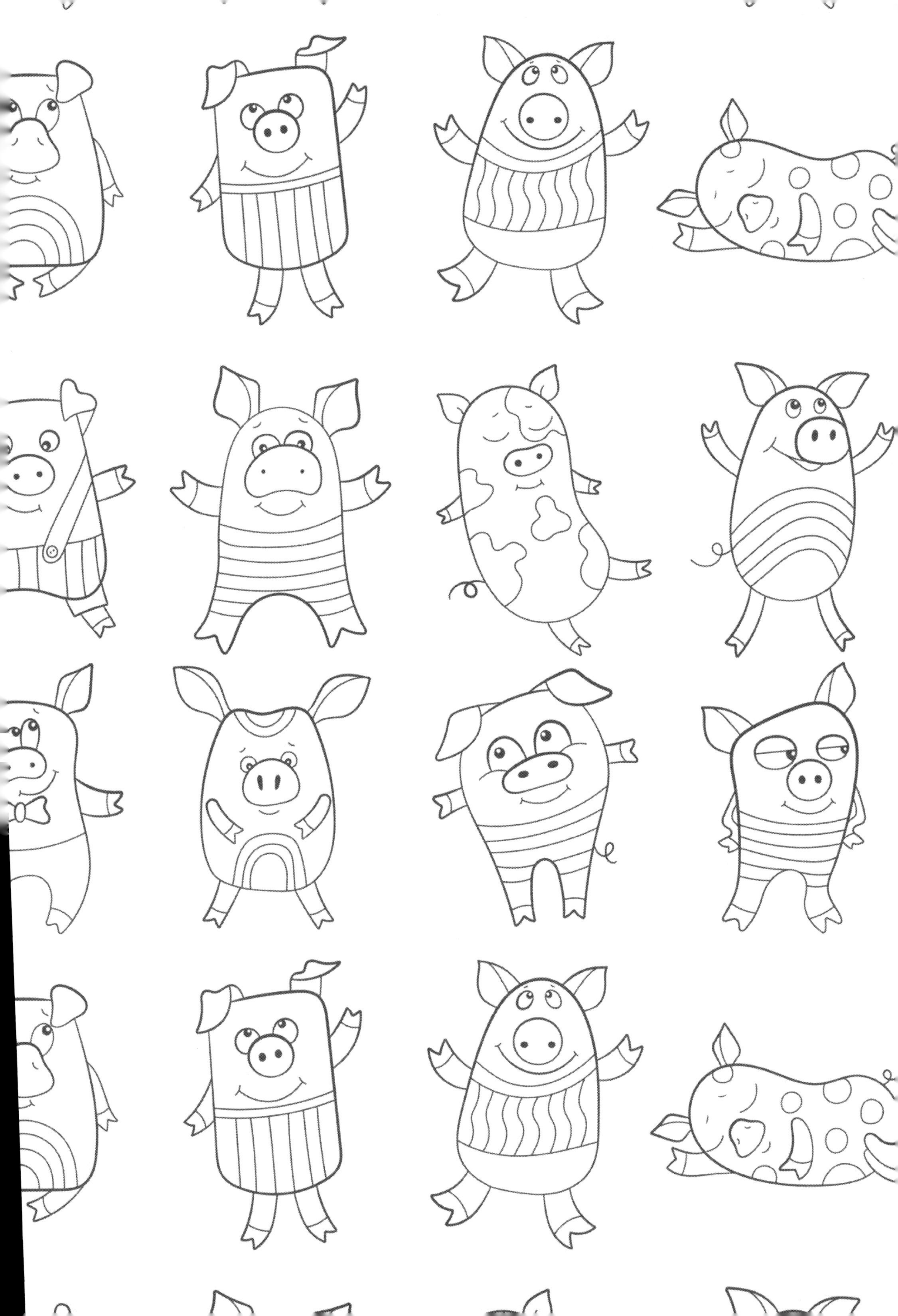

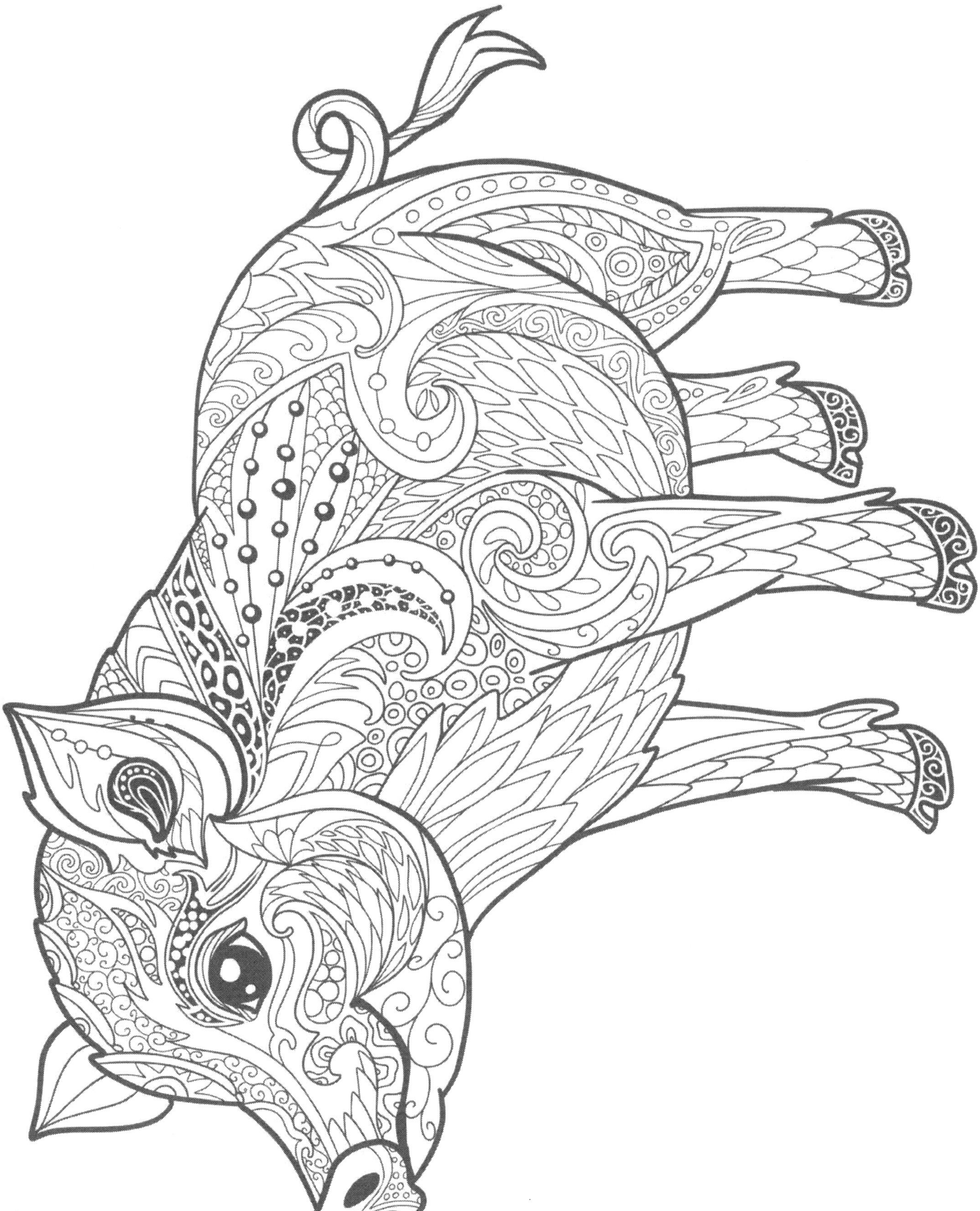

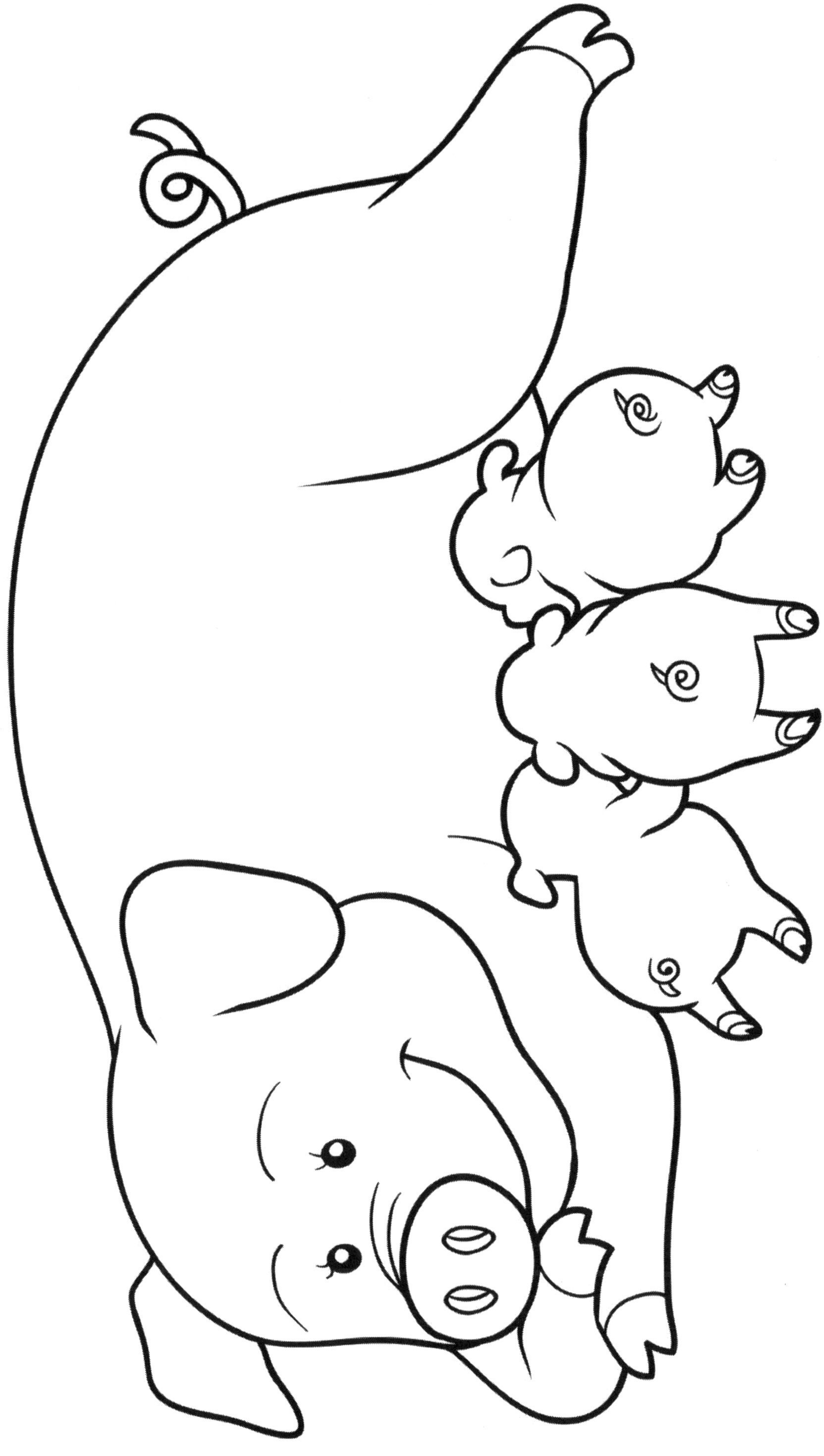

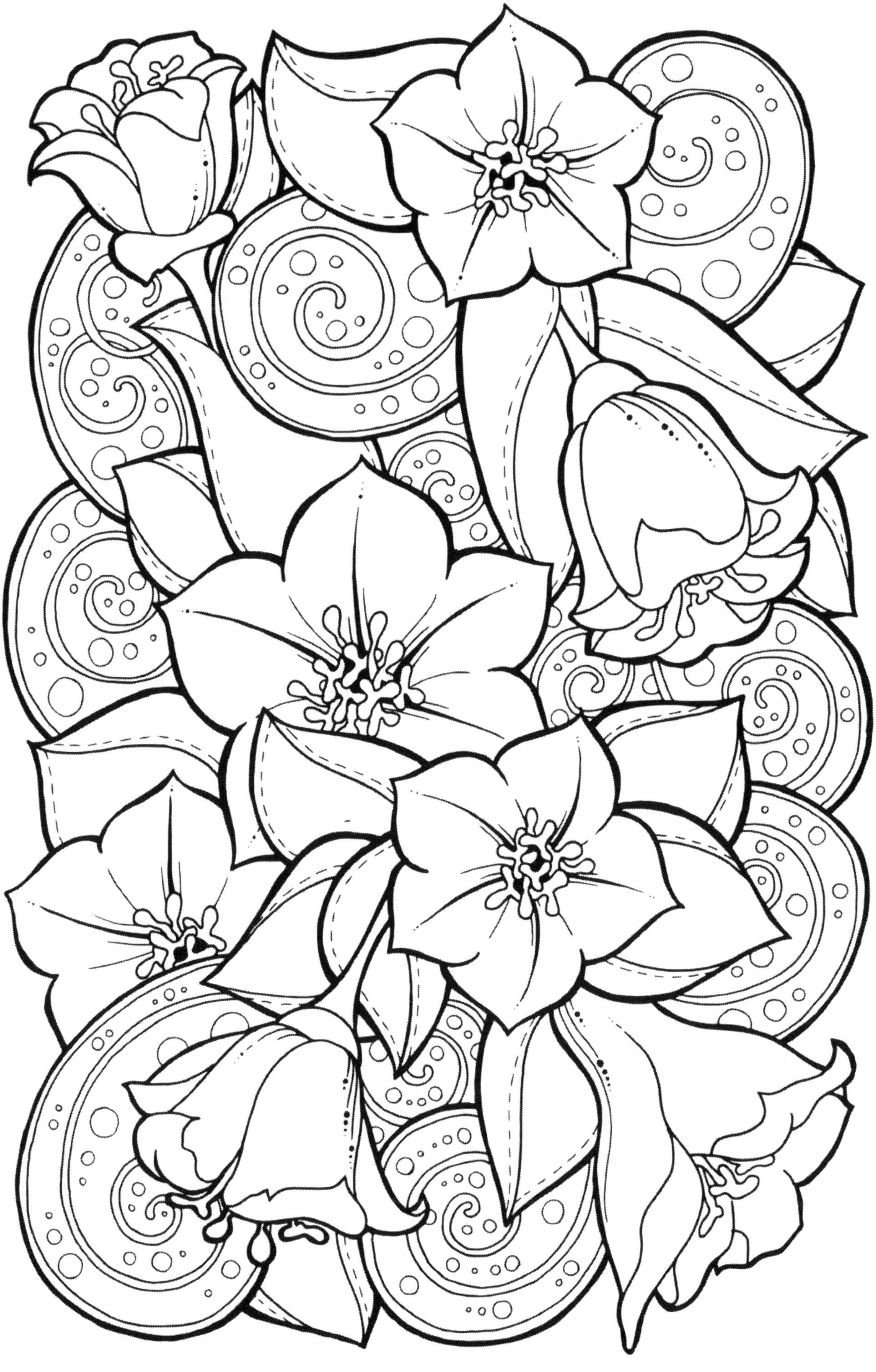

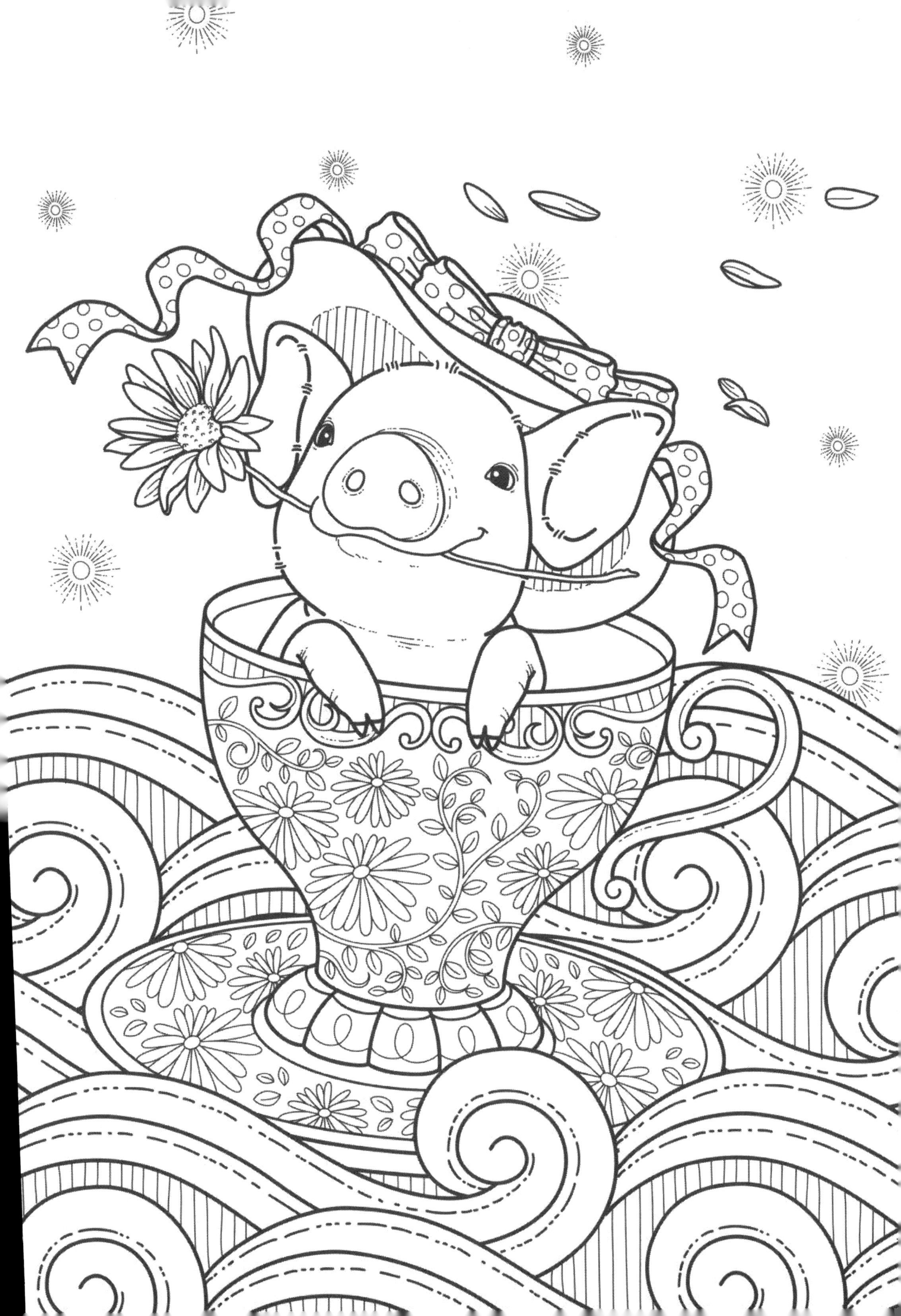

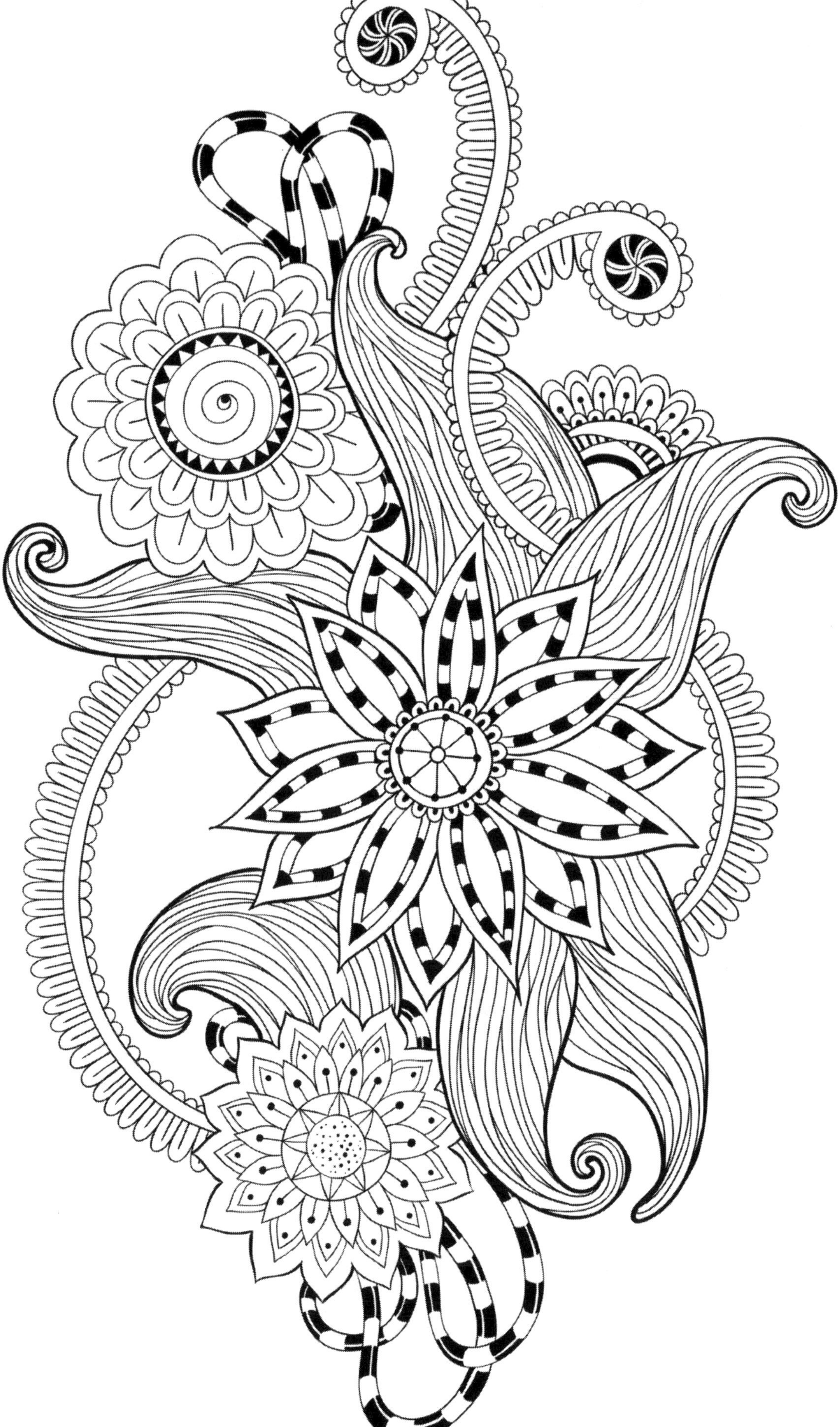

73950281R00031

Made in the USA
San Bernardino, CA
11 April 2018